Bark Beetle Symposium Participants

Snowbird, UT, November 15 – 18, 2005

Barbara Bentz, *Editor and Co-organizer*, US Forest Service (USFS) Rocky Mountain Research Station

Jesse Logan, *Co-organizer*, USFS Rocky Mountain Research Station
Jim MacMahon, *Facilitator*, Ecology Center, Utah State University

Craig D. Allen, US Geological Survey (USGS) New Mexico
Matt Ayres, Dartmouth College
Ed Berg, US Fish and Wildlife Service (USFWS) Alaska
Allan Carroll, Canadian Forest Service, British Columbia
Matt Hansen, USFS Rocky Mountain Research Station
Jeff Hicke, University of Idaho
Linda Joyce, USFS Rocky Mountain Research Station
Wallace Macfarlane, GeoGraphics, Inc., Utah
Steve Munson, USFS Forest Health Protection
Jose Negrón, USFS Rocky Mountain Research Station
Tim Paine, University of California at Riverside
Jim Powell, Utah State University
Ken Raffa, University of Wisconsin
Jacques Régnière, Canadian Forest Service, Quebec
Mary Reid, University of Calgary
Bill Romme, Colorado State University
Steven J. Seybold, USFS Pacific Southwest Research Station
Diana Six, University of Montana
Diana Tomback, University of Colorado, Denver
Jim Vandygriff, USFS Rocky Mountain Research Station
Tom Veblen, University of Colorado
Mike White, Utah State University
Jeff Witcosky, USFS Forest Health Protection
David Wood, University of California at Berkeley

Staff

Hannah Nordhaus, writer
Mitchelle Stephenson, design

Acknowledgments

We thank Stephanie White, Paige Weed, Ryan Davis, Donovan Gross, and Greta Schen for assistance at the workshop and in manuscript preparation. Neil Cobb, Dave Breshears, and Cynthia Melcher provided helpful comments on the manuscript. For assistance with aerial overflight data of bark beetle impacts we thank Jeanine Paschke, Gurp Thandi, and GeoGraphics, Inc. Elizabeth Grossman assisted with an early version of the manuscript. Funding was provided by the USDA Forest Service Rapid Science Assessment Team.

Report Highlights

Since 1990, native bark beetles have killed billions of trees across millions of acres of forest from Alaska to northern Mexico. Although bark beetle infestations are a regular force of natural change in forested ecosystems, several of the current outbreaks, which are occurring simultaneously across western North America, are the largest and most severe in recorded history.

There are many species of bark beetles, but only a few are responsible for the large areas of dead trees we see today. These species colonize live and recently downed trees, and kill either the entire tree or a portion of it during colonization and brood production. Bark beetle ecology is complex and dynamic, and a variety of circumstances must coincide for a bark beetle outbreak to succeed on a large scale. Only when specific conditions are met—ranging from suitable climatic conditions across an entire region, to the particular forest structure and age, to the existence of certain bacteria and fungi within the beetle and host tree—will bark beetle populations grow large enough to infest and kill trees across large landscapes.

> **A bark beetle outbreak requires:**
> - Abundant suitable host trees
> - A climate favoring bark beetle survival and development

Although outbreak dynamics vary from species to species and from forest to forest, the combination of two major factors appears to be driving the current outbreaks.

- Changing climatic conditions, in particular elevated temperatures and drought: elevated temperatures can speed up bark beetle reproductive and growth cycles and reduce cold-induced mortality during cold snaps. Extreme or prolonged water stress, caused by a combination of drought and warm temperatures, can weaken trees, making them more susceptible to bark beetle attacks.

- Forest history and host susceptibility: many conifer forests in western North America contain dense concentrations of large, mature trees that are highly susceptible to bark beetle outbreaks. The factors that have contributed to these conditions vary in relative importance from area to area. They include large stand-replacing fires (both natural and human-set) and timber harvesting near the end of the 19th century—disturbances that resulted in large areas of forest of similar size and age. In some areas, fire suppression over the last century also has inhibited the growth of new trees and created more dense stands. Because aggressive bark beetles favor mature trees, older, even-aged stands that have regrown or been replanted after disturbance events such as wildfire and harvesting may be more vulnerable to future bark beetle outbreaks than younger, more diverse stands. When trees must compete for resources in crowded conditions caused by either natural or human processes, bark beetles can more easily overcome stressed trees' defenses and initiate a severe outbreak.

Given the complexity of bark beetle community dynamics and the specific ecosystems they inhabit, the roles these factors play differ from forest to forest. Although research has uncovered a great deal of information about the life cycles and host interactions of some species of bark beetles, many gaps in our knowledge remain. In addition, because changing climate and forest disturbances have altered outbreak dynamics in recent years, some of what has been learned from past outbreaks may no longer hold true. There may be no equivalent in the 100 or so years of recorded history for the current outbreaks.

These recent infestations may result in dramatic changes to the long-term ecological pathways of some ecosystems, radically shifting vegetation patterns in some hard-hit forests. The visual landscape cherished by many nearby landowners and visitors is altered as well, as once-green trees turn brown and then lose their needles. In addition, bark beetle-killed trees pose some hazards when dead trees fall in areas of forest that humans frequent.

Although there are no known management options to prevent the spread of a large-scale bark beetle outbreak, land-use activities that enhance forest heterogeneity at the regional scale—such as creating patches of forest that contain diverse species and ages of trees—can reduce susceptibility to bark beetle outbreaks. However, because resource objectives often differ, and because the factors influencing a bark beetle outbreak vary depending on the species, host tree, local ecosystem, and geographical region, there is no single management action that is appropriate across all affected forests.

PHOTO BY JANE PARGITER, ECOFLIGHT, ASPEN CC

A whitebark pine forest in Bridger–Teton National Forest. The red trees were attacked and killed by mountain pine beetles the year before the photo was taken in July 2007.

IN THIS REPORT:

Introduction

Travel through a western North American forest today, and you will probably notice large areas of standing dead trees with dry reddish-brown needles, or ghostly gray snags from which all the needles have fallen. Across the West, from Alaska to Canada, throughout the Rocky Mountain region and the southwestern United States, many forests and hillsides are now blanketed with trees that have been recently infested and killed by various species of bark beetles.

New outbreaks of mountain pine beetle in British Columbia and Alberta are a sign of expansion beyond the beetle's recorded historical range.

These outbreaks of aggressive bark beetles, which are occurring in numerous forest ecosystems across western North America, are the biggest in recorded history. The term "aggressive" describes those species that can kill either the entire tree or a portion of it during colonization and brood production. Although western forests have experienced regular infestations throughout their history, the current outbreaks are remarkable for their intensity, their extensive range, and their simultaneous occurrence in multiple ecosystems across the continent.

These beetles are not only attacking forests where they have traditionally been found, but they also are thriving in some places where widespread infestations have not previously been recorded. Some outbreaks reflect the expansion of at least one bark beetle species beyond its recorded historical range.

With so many forests severely affected, land owners, land managers, policymakers, and the general public have taken notice. The extraordinary extent of the outbreaks has prompted concern that this massive loss of trees may impair ecosystem functioning and reduce the ability of our forests to provide future wildlife habitat, to protect watershed quality, to store carbon, and to be a source of timber and recreational opportunities.

Are the current bark beetle outbreaks unprecedented?

Q & A

Because it is technically difficult to reconstruct bark beetle outbreaks before the late 1800s, we are uncertain how extensive or severe outbreaks may have been prior to that time. However, scientists have examined outbreak frequency and severity over the last few centuries by examining tree-ring growth patterns, and made inferences about bark beetle presence in forest ecosystems prior to the last few centuries using ancient pollen and bark beetle remains. They also use computer models that describe how bark beetles respond to temperature to analyze beetle behavior in the past and compare it to current outbreaks. In doing so, they hope to answer two questions.

1) Is the scale of the current outbreaks—in terms of both geographic extent and the diversity and number of affected ecosystems—different from previously recorded outbreaks?

2) Have the underlying dynamics and mechanisms of bark beetle systems been altered because of new inputs to the forest systems in which bark beetles live? For instance, have a warming climate, air pollution, and/or historical patterns of forest management and fires altered forest habitat and beetle dynamics, allowing beetle populations to explode in recent years?

Why are these unusual bark beetle outbreaks occurring across western North America, and what will they do to our forests? In November 2005, scientists with the USDA Forest Service, Rocky Mountain Research Station convened a conference in Snowbird, Utah. Entomologists, ecologists, and foresters from across the continent shared the latest research on bark beetle outbreaks and sought to explain the causes, historical context, and short- and long-term consequences of the current outbreaks.

This publication is a product of that workshop. It first explains how bark beetles function within their native ecosystems, and then examines the

Mountain pine beetle–killed lodgepole pine.

recent outbreaks and explains how they differ from previous recorded infestations. Finally, the report explores the ecological effects of the current outbreaks and identifies areas where more research may be needed so we better understand the causes and consequences of current and future infestations.

The current bark beetle outbreaks differ from previously recorded infestations because of:

Their intensity — bark beetles are killing trees in larger numbers, at a faster pace, and over longer time periods

Their extent — bark beetle outbreaks are occurring in numerous ecosystems from Alaska to northern Mexico

Their synchroneity — bark beetle outbreaks are occurring concurrently across western North America

Bark Beetle Ecology and Biology

Native insects, including bark beetles, are among the greatest forces of natural change in forested ecosystems of North America. Every few decades, depending on weather and local forest conditions, bark beetle populations increase and infest large areas of conifer forest. In doing so, they play an essential role in forests' natural cycle of growth and regeneration.

A Source of Forest Renewal

Historically, bark beetles have not "destroyed" forests; rather, they have served as positive forces of transformation that redistribute nutrients and growing space. Whereas older trees often die en masse during bark beetle outbreaks, younger trees are usually not attacked. Released from competition for light, nutrients, and water, the young trees grow quickly to replenish the forest canopy. Thus, bark beetles can help mature forests regenerate. However, our understanding of the role bark beetles play in forests is based on observations from the past few centuries. As climate and local ecosystems change, the balance between bark beetles and their host forests also may change.

Bark beetles don't just kill trees; they also have beneficial effects. For example, certain lodgepole pine cones require heat from forest fires, which are sometimes fueled by beetle-killed trees, to release the seeds within. In addition, because beetles generally attack larger trees, they serve an essential regenerative function—they help renew forests by killing older and declining trees, allowing younger, more productive trees to compete successfully for light, nutrients, and water.

PHOTO BY J.M. MILLER   PHOTO BY M. FURNISS

These photos show the same Tenaya Creek drainage in Yosemite National Park. The photo on the left was taken in 1925, five years after a 1920 mountain pine beetle outbreak. The photo on the right, from 1984, shows how forests regenerate after beetle attacks.

Aggressive Bark Beetle Species, Hosts, and Habitats

Of the hundreds of different North American bark beetle species, only a handful of species (fewer than one percent) are considered aggressive, meaning the beetles kill all or a portion of the host trees they infest. These few species are primarily responsible for the large areas of tree mortality we see across the major forest ecosystems of western North America, from the spruce forests of the far North to the pine forests of the southwestern U.S.

The tree-killing bark beetles reside in a single family of insects (Curculionidae, subfamily Scolytinae), and each species has evolved to feed and reproduce in a single conifer group (Table 1). The Douglas-fir beetle, for instance, is found exclusively in Douglas-fir trees across western North America. The mountain pine beetle attacks and reproduces in at least 12 different species of North American pine across a number of ecosystems, from sea level to 10,000 feet in elevation, from the Pacific coast to the Black Hills of South Dakota, and from Baja California to central British Columbia. Its range has historically been limited by climate, not by the availability of host trees. For instance, although lodgepole pine trees are found as far north as northern British Columbia, western Alberta, and the Yukon and Northwest Territories, those areas until very recently had been untouched by mountain pine beetle. In recent years, however, mountain pine beetle outbreaks have been recorded in northern British Columbia and western Alberta; lodgepole pine forests in the Yukon and Northwest Territories still appear to be free of mountain pine beetles.

TABLE 1.

Aggressive Bark Beetles and their Host Trees in the Western U.S. and Canada

COMMON NAME	SCIENTIFIC NAME	MAJOR HOST TREE SPECIES IN THE U.S AND CANADA
mountain pine beetle	*Dendroctonus ponderosae*	lodgepole pine, ponderosa pine, bristlecone pine, whitebark pine, western white pine, sugar pine, limber pine, and others
spruce beetle	*Dendroctonus rufipennis*	Engelmann spruce, white spruce, Lutz spruce, Sitka spruce
Douglas-fir beetle	*Dendroctonus pseudotsugae*	Douglas-fir
western pine beetle	*Dendroctonus brevicomis*	ponderosa pine, Coulter pine
southern pine beetle	*Dendroctonus frontalis*	Apache pine, Chihuahua pine, ponderosa pine
Arizona fivespined ips	*Ips lecontei*	ponderosa pine
piñon ips	*Ips confusus*	piñon pine
western balsam bark beetle	*Dryocoetes confusus*	subalpine fir
fir engraver	*Scolytus ventralis*	white fir, California red fir, grand fir

PHOTO BY DANIEL RYERSON
Adult piñon ips beetles are only 0.12 to 0.14 inches long—barely larger than a grain of rice. Mountain pine beetles are slightly larger, around 0.20 inches, while spruce beetles average 0.22 inches long.

Ponderosa pines generally are found at lower elevations.

Species within the genus *Ips*, such as the piñon ips and Arizona fivespined ips, also can kill their hosts, although typically they are not considered major disturbance agents. In recent years, however, elevated population levels of a number of *Ips* species have coincided with drought, resulting in large areas of mortality, particularly in piñon and ponderosa pine forests of the southwestern U.S.

PHOTO BY SANDY KEGLEY

Whitebark pines are found at higher elevations in the northern Rocky Mountains of the U.S. and in the Canadian Rocky Mountains, as well as in Oregon, Washington, and California.

Life Cycle and Life Stages of a Bark Beetle

Native North American bark beetles in the genera *Dendroctonus, Dryocoetes, Ips,* and *Scolytus* live, feed on and lay their eggs in the soft living tissue of a tree, known as the phloem, which lies just below the tree's protective outer bark layer. These small beetles are ⅛ to ¼ inch long, dark brown to black, and cylindrical in shape. Bark beetle larvae, which develop from eggs laid inside the tree, are white and less than ¼ inch long, thus resembling a grain of rice. After maturing through four life stages—egg, larva, pupa, and adult—they emerge as new adults from the host tree and fly to a new live tree, where they mate and lay eggs to begin the cycle again (Figure 1).

Bark beetle life cycles range from a few weeks to two or three years, depending on the species and climate in which the beetles are found. Adult beetles attack their host trees during the time of year when they are most vulnerable—for example, spruce, true fir, and Douglas-fir trees are less able to fend off a beetle attack when their roots are still under snow. Bark beetles typically attack these trees in late spring, when air temperatures have warmed but snow remains on the ground.

Once a beetle finds and successfully burrows into a new tree, it builds chambers or shallow tunnels, known as "galleries," in which the female beetles lay their eggs. Each female can lay up to 200 tiny white or cream-colored eggs, which hatch within one to three weeks. After egg hatch, the larvae tunnel around the circumference of the tree, feeding as they go and impeding the flow of water and nutrients between the tree's roots and needles in the crown. Larvae of some species (e.g., southern pine beetle and western pine beetle) tunnel into the outer bark to complete development. Fungi introduced into a tree by bark beetles also may aid in tree death.

Bark beetle eggs. Most adult bark beetles chew a vertical or winding egg gallery in an infested tree and then lay their eggs in individual niches along the length of the gallery.

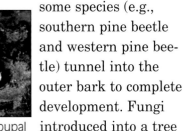

Bark beetle pupae. The pupal resting state is an intermediate stage that each beetle passes through as it goes from larva to adult.

Although the needles of an infested tree remain green for months after the initial attack, once a sufficient number of attacking adult beetles have initiated galleries and laid eggs, the tree has little chance of surviving. Following attack, the tree's needles turn yellow, orange, then red, and finally brown over a one- to two-year period. Eventually the needles drop to the forest floor. The length of time the dead tree remains standing depends on tree

PHOTO BY SCOTT TUNNOCK, USDA FOREST SERVICE, WWW.FORESTRYIMAGES.ORG

Mountain pine beetle larvae burrow horizontally across the host tree, eating phloem as they go. Other bark beetle species have winding galleries.

FIGURE 1.
Life Stages of a Bark Beetle

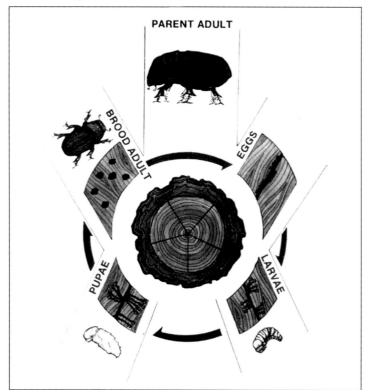

Bark beetles develop through four stages—egg, larva, pupa, and adult, before emerging to fly and attack another tree.

Trees turn reddish-orange within a year after bark beetle infestation, then brown and eventually gray as the needles fall to the ground.

species and locale. A typical beetle-killed lodgepole pine will fall to the ground within five to 10 years. Decomposition takes place more slowly in extremely arid climates—a number of high-

Whitebark pine killed by mountain pine beetle, most likely in the late 1920s.

elevation whitebark pines killed during a late 1920s mountain pine beetle outbreak in central Idaho, for instance, still remain standing today.

Bark Beetles and Temperature

Bark beetles, like all insects, are "ectotherms," and thus their development, survival, and reproductive success are highly temperature-dependent. Temperature influences everything in a bark beetle's life, from the number of eggs laid by a female to the beetle's ability to disperse to new host trees.

All western bark beetles have specific, evolved responses to temperature that can differ dramatically from species to species, and even within species. Most research on temperature-dependency in western North American bark beetles has been conducted with mountain pine beetle and spruce beetle. Although the general relationships described here may apply to other species, the specific details apply only to these two species.

FIGURE 2.

Mountain Pine Beetle Temperature Thresholds for Development in Central Idaho

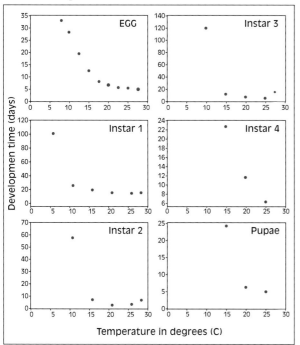

Mountain pine beetles develop to the next life stage only when enough thermal energy has accumulated and temperatures reach a certain threshold. These temperature thresholds and thermal energy requirements differ depending on geographic location, and help the beetles avoid cold-induced mortality during the sensitive egg and pupal stages. They also help to synchronize adult emergence.

From early in a bark beetle's life, temperature regulates the rate of development, determining when the insect moves from one life stage to the next (Figure 2). Different species—and even different populations within species with large geographical ranges—respond to different temperature thresholds. Mountain pine beetles, for instance, move into the next life stage only when enough thermal energy has accumulated and temperatures surpass a certain set threshold, which varies depending on location.

Those in the northern portion of the mountain pine beetle's range develop faster, and move into the pupal and adult life stages only when temperatures have risen above 15 degrees Celcius (C). This reduces the risk of cold-induced mortality and ensures emergence during summer months when air temperatures have warmed, and when some species of host trees are more vulnerable to attack. In southern climates, pupation appears to occur at cooler temperatures, an adaptation that synchronizes populations with the warmer environment. Other species, such as the spruce beetle, maintain synchrony by going into a resting state called "diapause," and resume their development only after detecting specific cues, such as temperature thresholds and/or longer periods of daily warming of the tree bark by solar radiation.

Temperature and Beetles

Temperature influences everything in a bark beetle's life, from how it develops, to how quickly it reproduces, to how long it lives. Colder temperatures keep beetle populations in check through cold-induced mortality and longer reproductive cycles. When temperatures warm, beetle populations in colder climates thrive.

Temperature is also a limiting factor in mountain pine beetle survival. Low temperature extremes, especially at certain times of the year when beetles are particularly sensitive, can result in widespread beetle mortality. To reduce cold-induced losses, the beetles' development is timed to progress through the egg and pupal stages, the most cold-susceptible stages, during warmer weather (Figure 3). The insects also generate "antifreeze" compounds that circulate through their bodies and help them survive in colder locales. Although bark beetles are well-adapted to cold winters, unusual cold snaps in the spring and fall may occur when antifreeze concentrations are low, thus resulting in widespread mortality.

Finally, temperature influences how quickly beetles complete a generation, and thus how often they reproduce. Whereas many bark beetle species that live in warmer, lower-elevation forests can develop numerous generations in a single year ("mulitvoltine") or one generation in a single year ("univoltine"), beetles that live at higher elevations, where weather is harsher and warm periods are shorter, most often reproduce on a less frequent "semivoltine" schedule, producing one generation every two years. Recent increases in temperature and growing-season length at higher elevations, however, have shifted many semivoltine, cold-weather-adapted beetles to a univoltine life cycle, resulting in rapid population growth.

Warming temperatures, combined with exceptionally susceptible host trees of similar age classes or weakened by crowding, drought, or old age, are believed to be a significant driver of large spruce beetle outbreaks in Alaska, Utah, and Colorado. Warmer temperatures also appear to be a factor in mountain pine beetle outbreaks in lodgepole pine forests of British Columbia and Colorado, and in high-elevation white pine forests throughout the northern and central Rocky Mountains.

Bark Beetle Flight and Pheromone Plumes

As described above, temperature determines the developmental timing of each life stage beneath the bark. Temperature also plays a role in the timing of adult emergence from trees and beetle flight. Once summer temperatures have warmed to approximately 16 °C to 18 °C, newly developed adults of most species begin a brief period of maturation feeding and then chew through the bark and fly to a new tree, synchronizing their emergence to attack their new hosts en masse.

FIGURE 3.
Phloem Temperature of Lodgepole Pine in Central Idaho

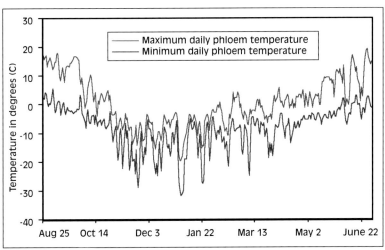

Mountain pine beetle live and feed in pine-tree phloem, a thin layer that lies just beneath the outer bark. The beetles live within the phloem for an entire year, and survive exposure to sub-freezing temperatures in the fall, winter, and spring by generating "antifreeze" compounds.

Beetles find their host trees based on a combination of factors: some appear to land randomly on new trees, whereas others seem to select their hosts based on either a visual assessment of size, or certain odors. Because larger trees provide an easier target and often have thicker phloem that allows female beetles to produce more offspring, aggressive bark beetles are more likely to attack large trees than small, young trees. *Ips* species are an exception, often attacking and killing small trees.

Although the exact mechanism is not known, scientists suspect that beetles most likely fly randomly until they encounter a "pheromone plume" that has been released by "pioneer" beetles that have selected a specific tree for attack. The process of chewing through the bark and ingesting tree phloem causes the synthesis of an attractive odor (pheromone) within the insects' guts. This odor can attract thousands of beetles to the same tree within a few days. As more beetles attack, more pheromone is produced. This is critical to the success of bark beetle attacks, as large numbers of beetles are required to overwhelm a tree's defenses. Once the tree is saturated with adult beetles, the attractive pheromone dissipates, repellant odors may be produced, and the tree no longer attracts additional beetles.

There are a number of factors that determine how far the beetles travel. Bark beetles prefer dense stands with tree canopies that touch, keeping attractant pheromones under the canopy where beetles can detect them. By flying below the tree tops but above the underbrush, they can best encounter pheromones emitted by other beetles. If there are no suitable host trees in a stand, the beetles will disperse farther and move into new areas to find susceptible trees. If the stand is very open and receives more heat and sunlight, the pheromones dissipate. Without pheromone attractants within the stand of trees, the beetles move up above the canopy, where they are often picked up by wind drafts and carried passively into other areas.

Wind currents can carry beetles above the forest canopy for many miles. For instance, recent infestations in northern Alberta, where 20th century mountain pine beetle outbreaks have not been recorded previously, are believed to have been started by beetles carried on upper air currents from infested areas in British Columbia. In the U.S., transport of infested logs from bark beetle-infested areas to those without active populations also may contribute to the long-distance movement of bark beetles.

Bark Beetles and Trees

How does a tiny beetle kill something as big as a tree?

Through sheer numbers: the more beetles that attack a tree, the easier it is to kill it. Trees do have defenses against bark beetle attacks. They produce a sticky, sap-like substance called resin

Overcoming a tree's defenses

Trees have natural defenses against beetle attacks. These can be overcome when:

1. trees are weakened by drought, disease or excessive competition
2. a large beetle population develops in the vicinity and attacks en masse, overwhelming even healthy trees

Trees respond to bark beetle attack by releasing a resin that is toxic to the invading beetles. If the tree is vigorous and few beetles are attacking simultaneously, it can survive an attack.

that contains toxic defensive chemicals. If a tree is healthy and vigorous and the number of beetles attacking is small, the tree can produce enough resin to kill the attacking beetles and fend off the attack. These defensive mechanisms, however, can be exhausted if many beetles attack the same tree within a few days.

Although many trees may be "suitable" for bark beetle infestations, not all are "susceptible" to attack. The most suitable trees—those whose thick phloem provides the best food for developing larvae—are generally healthy trees that have received adequate water, light, and nutrients. They often can resist the onslaught of a relatively small number of bark beetles. Susceptible trees, by contrast, are often unhealthy and easily overcome by even a small number of beetles, but often do not provide a good resource for larval feeding and survival. A number of factors—drought, tree diseases, and overcrowding—can make trees more vulnerable to beetle attacks, and in some cases bark beetles may infest weakened trees already doomed to die.

In general, dense, older stands, where trees must compete for resources, are more susceptible to bark beetle outbreaks, whereas heterogeneous landscapes that contain many sizes, ages, and species of trees are more resistant and resilient. Because less-crowded forests foster healthier trees, and because increased sunlight and wind in open tree canopies help disperse the pheromones that encourage mass bark beetle attacks, some studies indicate that removal of trees, or thinning, may reduce susceptibility in some forest types.

Even the healthiest tree, however, can not withstand a mass attack, and the explosion in beetle numbers in recent years has made extensive outbreaks more likely, killing healthy and unhealthy trees alike. Although beetles rarely kill all of the trees in a forest, it may appear that way in the months before the

In 1997, an unusual wind event on the Routt National Forest blew down large swaths of Engelmann spruce across 25,000 acres. Spruce beetle populations multiplied in the downed trees and then attacked green trees outside of the blowdown area.

beetle-killed trees' discolored needles drop. In several recent outbreaks, however, more than 90 percent of suitable host trees were killed by bark beetles in some stands.

Large numbers of recently downed trees also can contribute to severe outbreaks of some bark beetle species, particularly the Douglas-fir beetle and spruce beetle. When live trees are blown down, their phloem can remain suitable for bark beetle development up to a year later, whereas the trees' resinous defenses are depleted quickly due to the loss of contact between roots and soil. Beetle population numbers increase within the downed trees, and emerging adults can then successfully attack surrounding live host trees. An unusual wind event in 1997 in spruce forests on the Routt Divide in Colorado created the largest known blowdown in the Rocky Mountain region, and spruce beetle population levels increased dramatically in some of the affected areas.

The Community Beneath the Bark

Upon colonizing a tree, each beetle brings with it an array of fungi, nematodes, bacteria, and mites. Although the ecological roles of many of these organisms are not well understood, it is known that most bark beetles are symbiotically associated with specific fungi that may be important for beetle survival. Mountain pine beetles, for example, transport two fungal species in specialized body structures called mycangia (Figure 4). These fungi travel with the beetles when they disperse, and then grow in the phloem and sapwood of trees attacked by the beetles. The fungi may aid in successful colonization of a tree, and developing beetle larvae and adults also feed on the fungi, which help the beetles to process tree nutrients and also may provide vital nutrients not found in tree phloem. Research suggests that the fungi are also critical for brood development. Mountain pine beetles developing with fungi are larger than those without fungi, a size difference that can mean an increase in egg production of up to 300 percent.

Many bark beetle species introduce symbiotically associated fungi into trees as they enter through the bark. The growing bark beetle larvae feed on the fungi, which give the phloem and sapwood a bluish tint.

Adult mountain pine beetles feed on fungal spores prior to emergence from the brood tree.

Natural enemies and competitors of bark beetles also are attracted to bark beetle-infested trees. A wide variety of predators and parasitoids exploit bark beetles' pheromone communication system to find and feed on beetles walking on the outer bark and within trees they have infested. These natural enemies, which include checkered beetles and many species of woodpeckers, help keep normal, low-level bark beetle populations in check. Other less aggressive phloem- and sapwood-feeding beetle species also may compete with aggressive bark beetle species for food resources.

FIGURE 4.

Bark Beetle Fungal Associates

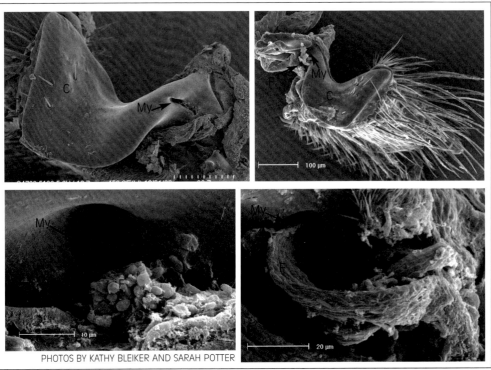

PHOTOS BY KATHY BLEIKER AND SARAH POTTER

Scanning electron micrographs showing the opening of the mycangia (My) of a mountain pine beetle, which is located on the maxillary cardine (C) near the mouth. The scanning electron micrographs show fungal material (F) protruding from the mycangia.

PHOTO BY VICKI SAAB

Three-toed woodpeckers feed on bark beetles and also make nests in trees the beetles kill.

PHOTO BY RYAN BRACEWELL

A checkered beetle eating an adult mountain pine beetle.

Over time, trees killed by bark beetles also are invaded by a number of other organisms, including wood-boring insects and rotting fungi, which are important in the tree's decay process. Once bark beetles have infested a tree, that tree becomes a veritable jungle of hitchhiking, predatory, and decay organisms.

Many bark beetle associates, in particular insect natural enemies and fungal species, are also sensitive to temperature, developing and reproducing when temperatures reach specific thresholds. It is not clear how climate warming may change the relationship between beetles and their hitchhiking fungal, predatory, and parasitic associates.

Bark Beetle Outbreaks

Written and tree-ring records dating back as far as 1750 indicate a consistent record of intermittent outbreaks of aggressive bark beetles in various forest types across the West. Over the past 10-15 years, however, the frequency, severity, and extent of bark beetle outbreaks have increased. Bark beetles have killed large numbers of trees in multiple forest ecosystems throughout their historical range, and also in some ecosystems where outbreaks have never or seldom been recorded (Figure 5).

Bark beetles are active in a number of different species of trees.

- Mountain pine beetles are killing large numbers of lodgepole pine in the Rocky Mountain region.

- Mountain pine beetles have been found in high elevation white pines, such as whitebark, bristlecone pine, and limber pine. These pines are generally long-lived, and are restricted to higher elevations throughout the West. They are considered foundation species, which play extremely important roles in the ecosystems where they are found and are vital to the survival of other local species.

- Mountain pine beetle outbreaks are occurring in northern lodgepole pine and lodgepole/jack pine hybrid forests in Alberta.

- Unusually large outbreaks of spruce beetles are occurring in Alaska, Utah, Washington, Wyoming, Arizona, Colorado, and the Yukon Territory.

- In the southwestern United States, *Ips spp.* beetles have killed extraordinary numbers of ponderosa and piñon pines.

- Western pine beetles have killed large numbers of ponderosa pine in southern California and throughout the southwestern U.S.

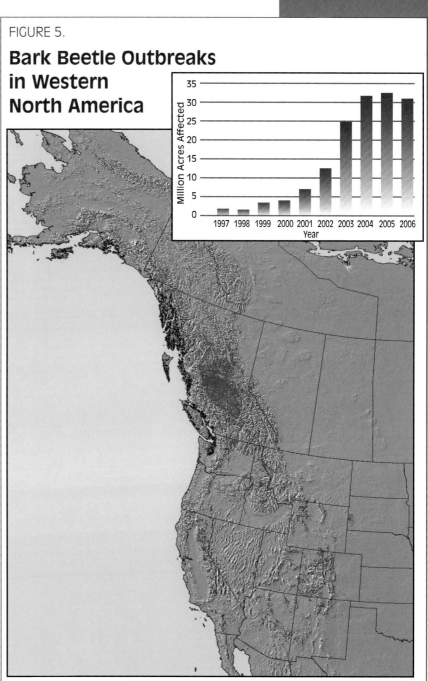

FIGURE 5.

Bark Beetle Outbreaks in Western North America

SOURCE: NATURAL RESOURCES CANADA, CANADIAN FOREST SERVICE; USDA FOREST SERVICE, FOREST HEALTH PROTECTION

Native bark beetles have affected more than 150 million acres of western North American forests during the past 10 years.

- Douglas-fir beetle, fir engraver, and western balsam bark beetle are active throughout the West.

- Southern pine beetle is active in pine forests of southern and central Arizona.

Over the past 120 years, forest rangers, land managers, and forest entomologists recorded outbreaks of many bark beetle species throughout the West. In 1934, **Chief Ranger George F. Baggley** and **Forester Maynard Barrows** wrote about a severe outbreak in Yellowstone National Park:

"The mountain pine beetle epidemic is threatening all of the white bark and lodgepole pine stands in Yellowstone Park. Practically every stand of white bark is heavily infested...and will be swept clean in a few years. If the insects spread from the white bark pine to the lodgepole stands, it seems inevitable that much of the park will be denuded."

— from "Montana's Thirty Year Mountain Pine Beetle Infestation," James C. Evenden, 1944.

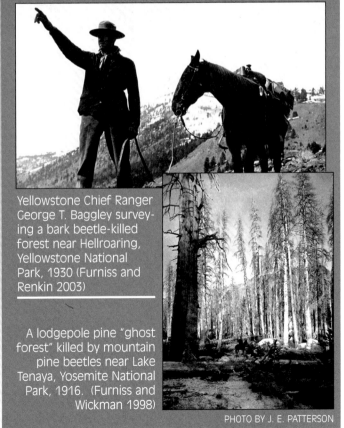

Yellowstone Chief Ranger George T. Baggley surveying a bark beetle-killed forest near Hellroaring, Yellowstone National Park, 1930 (Furniss and Renkin 2003)

A lodgepole pine "ghost forest" killed by mountain pine beetles near Lake Tenaya, Yosemite National Park, 1916. (Furniss and Wickman 1998)

PHOTO BY J. E. PATTERSON

Since 1997, bark beetles have collectively killed billions of trees across billions of acres of forest in western North America. The fact that so many regionwide bark beetle events are happening concurrently at such intensity across so many ecosystems is truly remarkable and suggests common factors.

Historical Bark Beetle Outbreaks

Are the current bark beetle attacks unprecedented? To understand the significance of the current outbreaks, scientists are using a variety of techniques to piece together the frequency, intensity, timing, area, and duration of previous beetle outbreaks and other forest disturbance events. Understanding bark beetles' historical range and variations in behavior over long periods of time is key.

We know that bark beetles have been associated with forests since at least the Holocene era, which began approximately 12,000 years ago, and probably much longer. Remains of *Dendroctonus* from 8000 years ago, for instance, were identified in lake sediment cores taken in the Bitterroot Mountains of Montana. More recently, forest rangers, land managers, and forest entomologists have recorded outbreaks of many species throughout the West. These early written records date back to the late 1880s and are qualitative in nature. For example, a forest ranger riding his horse across vast acres of forest might have noted that beetles had killed a large number of lodgepole pine in a certain drainage or forest.

Acquiring quantitative assessments of previous bark beetle outbreaks is more complicated. It is far more difficult to trace the history of a bark beetle outbreak than it is to understand fire history in many forest types. Although forest fires often spare many trees in a forest, leaving behind scars on surviving trees that scientists can detect in tree rings many years later, trees that have been mass-attacked by bark beetles do not live to tell the tale. It can be difficult to examine the cores of many species of beetle-killed trees, particularly in areas where decomposition occurs rapidly. In some dry, high elevation sites where decomposition occurs slowly, however—such as in high-elevation whitebark pine forests—scientists have been able to use tree rings of well-preserved, beetle-killed trees to date mountain pine beetle outbreaks as far back as the late 1880s.

In most instances, scientists must date outbreak events by looking for more subtle evidence in the rings of those trees that survived. Because bark beetles kill larger trees first, smaller trees in the vicinity of a beetle outbreak and/or non-host tree species often grow at a dramatically increased rate when freed from competition for light and water from larger trees nearby. Thus, a sudden and sustained increase—or "growth release"—in tree-ring width among a number of trees in a stand during the same period is an indication that the trees survived a major disturbance event. After factoring out the influence of climate—such as increased precipitation, which also can result in a wide growth ring—a bark beetle outbreak can be deduced (Figure 6).

Studies using these techniques suggest that spruce beetle and mountain pine beetle outbreaks have been regular occurrences in western North American forests in recent centuries. Tree ring analyses on the Kenai Peninsula in Alaska,

FIGURE 6.
Growth Release in Trees Surviving Bark Beetle Outbreaks

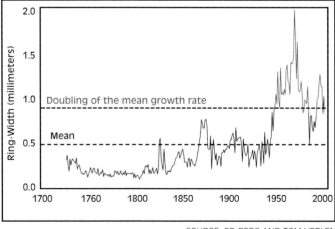

SOURCE: ED BERG AND TOM VEBLEN

Trees that survive bark beetle outbreaks often experience a "growth release" — a period of much faster growth that results in a doubling of tree-ring width over a ten-year period — after surrounding trees have been killed by bark beetles. Historical outbreaks can be dated by measuring growth releases in rings of trees that survived the outbreak. The rings of this tree provide evidence of an outbreak in 1942.

for example, suggest that spruce beetle outbreaks occurred frequently over the last 250 years, with a mean return interval of 52 years. Similar patterns were observed for spruce beetles in Colorado spruce forests and for mountain pine beetles in lodgepole pine forests of British Columbia.

Features of Current Bark Beetle Outbreaks

Current outbreaks appear to be different from observations of 20th century historical outbreaks because of these factors.

- Regional scale – simultaneous severe outbreaks of several species are occurring across the West
- Longer duration and intensity – some outbreaks are lasting longer and more trees are dying at a faster rate
- Extended range – mountain pine beetles are moving north and east beyond their previously recorded range
- New tree species – mountain pine beetles have been found reproducing in spruce and jack/lodgepole pine hybrids

Are the Current Outbreaks Different?

The history of bark beetle infestations varies from forest to forest and ecosystem to ecosystem, making generalization difficult. Research into past outbreaks, however, suggests that the current infestations may be more severe and widespread than previous outbreaks due to a number of factors.

Regional scale: Although large outbreaks previously occurred in forested systems across the West, the historical evidence suggests that in the past century or two, there have not been so many concurrent outbreaks at such a broad scale involving so many species and locations simultaneously. This is particularly true for the mountain pine beetle and spruce beetle. Similar widespread outbreaks may have occurred farther back in geologic time, but we do not have the tools to precisely evaluate the extent of outbreaks that occurred so far in the past.

Longer duration and intensity: In several ecosystems, outbreaks are lasting longer than they typically did during the 20th century, and more trees are dying at a faster rate. We are seeing massive tree mortality in habitats where previously recorded outbreaks have been limited in duration and extent.

Extended range: Most bark beetles are limited in geographical spread to the range of host trees they attack. The spruce beetle for instance, can survive in all places where spruce trees currently exist. The mountain pine beetle's range, however, is bounded not by the trees it infests, but by climate. Lodgepole pine extends farther north than the traditional range of the mountain pine beetle that feeds on it, and ponderosa and other pine species grow farther south. Recently, however, mountain pine beetles have dispersed out of their historical range, extending farther north and east across Canada's Rocky Mountain crest (Figure 7). Currently, their range has not expanded to the south, despite the presence of suitable host trees.

New tree species: Although jack pine is not believed to be a historical host for mountain pine beetle, the insects have recently been found in jack pine/lodgepole pine hybrids on the east side of the Continental Divide in northern Alberta, Canada. In addition, mountain pine beetle has been found attacking and successfully reproducing in spruce trees in British Columbia and Colorado—the first evidence of multiple generations of mountain pine beetle in a non-pine species.

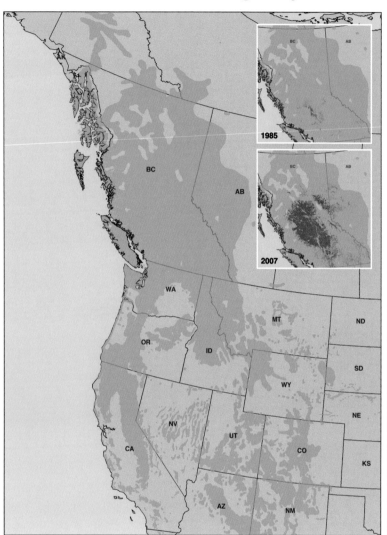

FIGURE 7.
Mountain Pine Beetle Range Expansion

SOURCE: NATURAL RESOURCES CANADA, CANADIAN FOREST SERVICE; USDA FOREST SERVICE, FOREST HEALTH PROTECTION

The range of the mountain pine beetle generally follows its major host pine species throughout western North America (shown in green). The mountain pine beetle's current range extends south to the tip of southern California and central Arizona near Flagstaff. In recent years, mountain pine beetle outbreak populations have been found farther north in British Columbia and east in northern Alberta than was observed in historical records, including those of the most recent large outbreak in 1985.

South-Central Alaska — A Spruce Beetle Outbreak That Ran Its Course

From 1987 to 1997, an unprecedented run of warm summers, combined with mature, dense forests, allowed spruce beetle populations in south-central Alaska to explode. By the end of that 10-year period, the spruce beetle had essentially exhausted the supply of large host trees. On the Kenai Peninsula, 1.6 million acres of forest were affected; greater south-central Alaska lost most of the mature trees across a 2.9-million-acre area.

Weather in the region is strongly influenced by the El Niño-La Niña cycle—when fluctuating Pacific Ocean temperatures alter weather patterns across the Western Hemisphere. In the past, several warm El Niño summers in a row could initiate an outbreak, which would then subside with the onset of several cool La Niña summers. Following 1987, however, summer temperatures increased about 2 °C on average. Temperatures did not drop below the mean, even during the weak La Niña summers of 1988-89 and 1996. Warm summers accelerated the spruce beetle's normal two-year life cycle to one year, providing a double dose of beetles the following spring. The warm weather also lengthened the growing season for host trees. Without a concomitant increase in precipitation, however, the trees became stressed and more susceptible to successful bark beetle colonization.

In addition to the unusually warm weather, the Kenai forests were especially susceptible because they were densely stocked with large, mature trees. With continuing warm temperatures enhancing spruce beetle development and survival, the only factor limiting the outbreak was the supply of suitable host trees in the area. Only when the supply of host trees had been exhausted did the outbreak collapse.

Will the overwhelming supply of dead trees in this large area of beetle-killed forests lead to additional or more intense forest fires in the area? Soil charcoal analyses suggest that the mean fire return interval in these forests is 400-600 years, while bark beetle outbreaks occur on average every 50 years, according to tree-ring evidence. Therefore, there is no evidence of any relationship between spruce beetle outbreaks and fire over the last 250+ years. The climate during this period was distinctly cooler, however, and today's warmer climate may intensify fire risk in both green and beetle-killed forests.

PHOTO BY DANIEL BELTRA/AFP/GETTY IMAGES

Spruce beetle outbreaks in south-central Alaska have essentially exhausted the supply of large host trees. On the Kenai Peninsula, 1.6 million acres have been affected.

Contributing Factors

Why are the recent outbreaks so severe and widespread? Scientists point to a number of factors contributing to the outbreaks. Many of these factors, such as rising temperatures, regionwide drought, and mature and over-mature forests, are in effect across large areas in numerous ecosystems. Specific conditions within particular forests or forest stands, however—such as the species and density of trees, along with local ecology and weather conditions—often preclude making broad generalizations.

Scientists do agree that the current outbreaks are taking place at a time when forests have been affected by a variety of human activities, and that certain basic dynamics appear to lie behind the current outbreaks. These include:

- a changing climate affecting all areas with bark beetle outbreaks;

- previous forest management practices such as selective timber harvesting and wildfire suppression in some forest types and some geographic areas;

- natural disturbances, such as climate-driven wildfire, that occurred in previous centuries; and

- other human influences on forest ecosystems such as pollution.

Climate

Because bark beetles are highly sensitive to slight changes in their environments, small shifts in one component of their ecology—such as climate—can create rapid and extreme shifts in outbreak dynamics. In recent years, the climate in which bark beetles develop has changed noticeably. The 11 years between 1995 and 2006, for instance, ranked among the warmest since record-keeping began in 1850; the current prolonged drought across the West is the longest in duration since at least 1900; atmospheric carbon dioxide has increased 30 percent over the last 150 years. All of these changes appear to have dramatic direct and indirect effects on beetle populations.

- **Direct Effects of Warming Temperature:** The increase in regional temperatures in recent years has permitted some species of bark beetle to extend their ranges to higher altitudes and latitudes. Warming temperatures in winter, fall, and spring also reduce cold-induced bark beetle mortality. Research suggests that the probability of mountain pine beetle survival during the past 10 to 20 years has increased as a result of elevated minimum temperatures at many locations.

  In addition, warmer temperatures have sped up the life cycles of some species of bark beetles, increasing the number of beetles, which can then more easily overcome a tree's natural defenses. In some high-elevation forests, spruce beetles, which typically produce one generation

> **Mature forests are the loaded gun for today's severe bark beetle infestations, and weather is the trigger.**

every two years, have shifted to one generation per year. Some high-elevation mountain pine beetles, as well, now produce a new generation in one year instead of two. In the southwestern U.S., it is believed that *Ips* species, fueled by higher temperatures, also have been reproducing at a faster rate. These population increases, in conjunction with drought, have caused massive piñon and ponderosa mortality in the Southwest. In Arizona, for instance, more than 6 million trees were killed across 1.2 million acres between 2001 and 2004.

- **Indirect Effects of Warming Temperature and Drought:** The current regionwide drought, in combination with elevated temperatures, has weakened trees throughout western North American forests. Although moisture stress can kill trees directly, severely moisture-stressed trees also may be more vulnerable to bark beetle attacks. The relationship between moisture stress and tree defense against bark bee-

Climate Change and Bark Beetles: The Perfect Storm

The West's changing climate—rising temperatures and decreasing precipitation—has created weather conditions that are ideal for bark beetle outbreaks.

- Because bark beetles are extremely sensitive to changes in temperature, recent rising temperatures have led to rapid population increases in some forests. Longer, warmer summers have extended reproductive and growth periods, while fewer cold snaps and higher winter temperatures have permitted increased bark beetle survival in winter, spring, and fall.

- Because most tree species are sensitive to water stress, warm regionwide droughts—such as the current prolonged drought across the West, the longest we have seen for over a century—weaken trees and make them more susceptible to bark beetle attacks. Forests full of drought-stressed trees, combined with rapidly expanding bark beetle populations, can combine to fuel exponential beetle population growth.

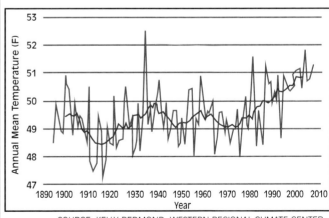

SOURCE: KELLY REDMOND, WESTERN REGIONAL CLIMATE CENTER
Annual January-December temperature in 11 western U.S. states. Blue line is an 11-year running average.

Piñon Ips in the Southwestern U.S.: Drought, Overgrowth, and Rising Temperatures

In the southwestern United States, the interaction between severe water stress and bark beetles has killed ponderosa and piñon pines on millions of acres since 2000. Although bark beetle outbreaks also occurred during the last severe drought in the Southwest region in the 1950s, piñon pine mortality has been particularly extreme during the recent drought.

PHOTO BY CRAIG D. ALLEN
Piñon pine mortality in the Jemez Mts. near Los Alamos, NM, October 2002.

Scientists believe there are two reasons for the current widespread dieback. First, southwestern forest stands are denser than they were 50 years ago. Historical livestock grazing and fire suppression, along with an unusually wet period in the Southwest from 1978 until the mid-1990s, promoted tree establishment and resulted in unusually dense forests and woodlands. Overcrowded, stressed trees are more vulnerable to bark beetle infestation, especially during dry conditions.

Second, although temperature patterns were not unusual during the 1950s drought, the recent 2000s drought has been associated with significantly higher temperatures. These warmer temperatures amplified water stress, in some cases causing direct piñon pine mortality, and

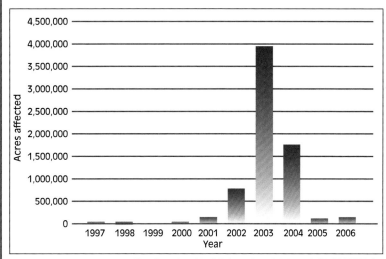

Piñon and Ponderosa Pine Mortality in the Southwestern U.S., 1997-2006

SOURCE: USDA FOREST SERVICE, FOREST HEALTH PROTECTION

Ips and western pine beetle affected more than 7 million acres of piñon and ponderosa pine in Colorado, Arizona, New Mexico, Nevada, and Utah between 1996 and 2005. Severe drought and increased temperature contributed to the widespread tree mortality.

also may have allowed Ips bark beetles to reproduce at a faster rate, increasing the number of generations that develop in a single year. The result is unprecedented tree mortality across extensive areas—95 percent of mature piñon pines have been killed in some forests of the southwestern U.S., with over 3 million acres affected by substantial piñon pine mortality.

This recent drought episode is an example of "global-change-type drought," where reduced precipitation, accompanied by increased temperatures, can result in extensive and rapid changes in vegetation. Climate models suggest that we will see more of this type of drought in the southwestern United States in coming years.

CASE STUDY

tle attack, however, is complex. Not every drought triggers a bark beetle outbreak, and different forest ecosystems respond differently to outbreaks triggered by moisture stress. In the southwestern piñon and ponderosa pines affected by the recent *Ips* and western pine beetle outbreaks, the return to more typical moisture levels also meant the end of the beetle outbreak. In the ongoing mountain pine beetle outbreak in British Columbia, however, beetle population growth and associated tree mortality continued even after drought conditions subsided.

> ## New Inputs
>
> Scientists believe a number of factors have changed the "inputs" to forest systems in which bark beetles are found, and have contributed to recent outbreaks. They include:
> - Rising temperatures
> - Prolonged drought
> - Air pollution
> - Previous forest management practices

Disturbance and Human Influence

- **Wildfire Suppression:** Since the early 20th century when the U.S. and Canadian governments implemented a policy to suppress all fires on federal land, many fire-prone ecosystems have experienced long fire-free intervals. In some cases, the species composition and structure of those forests have changed, creating dense forests full of the mature and over-mature trees bark beetles favor.

  Such shifts have taken place in low-elevation ponderosa pine forests in the southwestern United States, where once-parklike stands of trees, kept open by regular surface fires every two to 12 years, are now dense forests, and in lodgepole pine forests in British Columbia. Other ecosystems, however, such as subalpine spruce, fir, and lodgepole pine forests in Colorado, and whitebark pine forests in the northern Rocky Mountains, typically experience longer periods of time between fires. In many areas, current forest density does not appear to be a consequence of fire suppression over the last century.

  The role of fire suppression in bark beetle outbreak dynamics is a topic of much discussion among scientists, reflecting the need for additional research. Although the effect of fire suppression on bark beetle outbreaks varies by forest ecosystem, region, and the level of management applied, it is fair to conclude that in some cases, fire suppression policies may have helped create a landscape that is more susceptible to bark beetle attacks.

- **Disturbance history:** Bark beetle-caused tree mortality can be significant in forests where the majority of trees are the same species and are uniformly mature and large. Because aggressive bark beetles favor

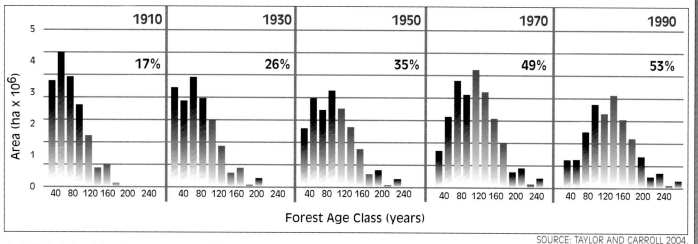

FIGURE 8.
Susceptible Lodgepole Pine Forests in British Columbia

SOURCE: TAYLOR AND CARROLL 2004.

In British Columbia, the percentage of lodgepole pine forest in age classes susceptible to mountain pine beetle (in red) is predicted to have increased from 17 percent of total forest area in 1910 to 53 percent in 1990. A century of fire suppression and forest management practices have helped create these forest conditions.

mature trees, stands that have regrown or been replanted after a distinct disturbance event, such as harvesting, wildfire, or previous bark beetle outbreaks, may be more vulnerable to future bark beetle outbreaks, especially when the majority of trees are competing for resources in overcrowded conditions. For instance, in British Columbia selective harvesting—along with fire suppression—has contributed to a predominance of mature stands that are highly susceptible to mountain pine beetle outbreaks (Figure 8). Not all disturbances create susceptible forests, however. Some fires, and even some timber harvesting, can reduce stand density and future susceptibility to bark-beetle outbreak initiation.

- **Air Pollution:** Local and long-distance dispersal of air pollution from heavily populated areas and increasing development on the edges of forests also can have an indirect influence on bark beetle outbreaks. Ozone can damage needles, disrupting the tree's photosynthetic capacity, thereby weakening the tree and making it more susceptible to bark beetle attack. An increase in atmospheric nitrogen deposition can stimulate growth in trees, leaving energy resources too depleted to produce sufficient resin to defend against bark beetle attack.

Are the current bark beetle outbreaks unprecedented?

Relative to what we know about the scale of historic outbreaks, many of the current bark beetle outbreaks do appear to be larger, more widespread, more severe, and occurring in new and novel habitats. This is, in part, due to the fact that the inputs to the system have changed, allowing bark beetles to thrive.

Q & A

The Future of Our Forest Ecosystems

While some bark beetle researchers comb through tree-ring, pollen, and fossil records to understand how and why current beetle outbreaks may differ from those in the past, others scientists have developed sophisticated simulation models to help predict bark beetle activity in the near and distant future.

These models use data gathered in the field and laboratory to describe the mechanics of bark beetle response to temperature. Such mechanistic models can then be used to predict how current and future temperature patterns may affect bark beetle outbreak dynamics on local and landscape scales (Figure 9). These temperature-based models have been developed only for the mountain pine beetle and spruce beetle. They do not yet predict dynamics of other aggressive bark beetle species, nor do they take into account variability in temperature response among mountain pine and spruce beetle populations across their ranges. To adequately predict the effect of changing climate on all forest ecosystems throughout western North America, scientists must develop models for other species, and refine the current models to take into account geographic variability within a species.

There is always a high degree of uncertainty in attempting to forecast the future, especially on a regional or global scale. Still, scientists can make informed estimates by using these sophisticated computer models, combined with an understanding of the underlying mechanisms of bark beetle response to temperature, to predict how those dynamics may adjust to changing conditions. The general consensus is that continued warming will fuel beetle attacks in areas where beetle activity was previously constrained by climate, such as in northern latitudes and at higher elevations. In locations where bark beetles are currently successful, however, continued warming could cause some beetle populations to go locally extinct unless they are able to rapidly adapt. If local populations of bark beetle die out due to warming, it is possible that other species could then move into those vacated niches. For example, aggressive species currently restricted to the southwest U.S. and Mexico could expand in range northward as the climate warms.

Ecological Consequences of Recent Bark Beetle Outbreaks

Bark beetles have, for millennia, been a natural part of the forest regeneration process. Bark beetles help to winnow out old and mature trees so that younger, more productive trees can replenish an aging forest. They also accelerate the process of tree decay to help forests capture and recycle nutrients. In recent years, however, a combination of factors, including warm temperatures, drought-stressed trees, susceptible landscapes, and historical management practices, may have tipped many systems out of the balance we have observed over the past century. Beyond the troubling sight of vast areas of dead trees scattered over large landscapes in western North American forests, scientists are concerned that the current levels and rates of tree mortality in some forest ecosystems may be pushing these systems beyond their ability to recover and regenerate.

Bark beetles can kill large numbers of trees in a forest within three to five years, yet many tree species require hundreds of years to reach maturity. Therefore, a massive beetle outbreak can create large shifts in vegetation types and patterns in affected forests. In a stand with several different species of trees, those tree species that are not attacked may now become the dominant vegetation—for instance, aspen or fir trees may take over after spruce trees die.

In stands that are composed predominantly of one species of similar age, a bark beetle outbreak can cause an even more dramatic shift in the type of vegetation found there.

PHOTO BY ED BERG

Grass invading areas on Alaska's Kenai Peninsula, where overstory spruce were killed by spruce beetle and subsequently removed by logging.

FIGURE 9.

Predicted Change in Bark Beetle Outbreak Probability with Warming Temperatures

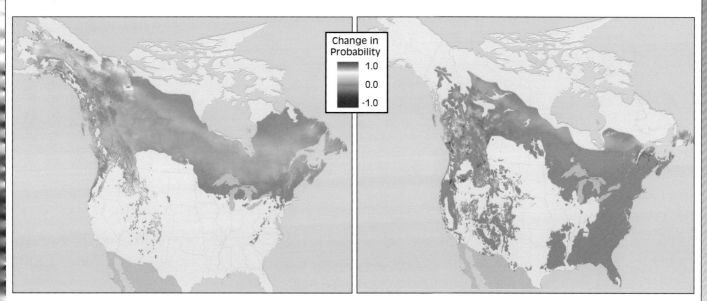

Temperature-driven model predictions suggest that over the next 30 years, spruce forests in Alaska, the Northwest Territories, and at high elevations in the western United States will see increased probability of univoltine life cycle spruce beetle. Higher temperatures are expected to speed up the life cycle of many spruce beetles from one generation every two years to one generation per year, resulting in exponential population growth and thus an increased likelihood of severe outbreaks (left). Over the same time period, the likelihood of population success in areas within the current range of mountain pine beetle (see Figure 7) is predicted not to change dramatically except in high elevation forests of the western U.S. and in northern British Columbia (right). Over the next 30 years, a low likelihood of mountain pine beetle range expansion is predicted in the central and eastern U.S. and Canada, areas where pine species grow but are outside the current range of mountain pine beetle.

CASE STUDY

Whitebark Pine in the Northern Rocky Mountains: Mountain Pine Beetle Outbreaks, Coupled with the Exotic Blister Rust Pathogen, Threaten Local Extinction

In the past 10 years, mountain pine beetles have infested and killed more than 570,000 acres of whitebark pine in the northern Rocky Mountains of the United States. Whitebark pine is a long-lived five-needle white pine that lives in the upper subalpine zone, tolerating harsh temperature and moisture extremes that many other conifers are not adapted to. Whitebark pine trees are vital to the survival of a number of wildlife species, such as red squirrels, black and brown bears, and Clark's nutcracker—the tree's principal seed disperser. Whitebark pine trees also can act as "nurse trees" for other species such as subalpine fir by providing shelter from the harsh, windy conditions. The trees grow higher in elevation than most conifers, and both stabilize soil and regulate snow melt in the treeline zone.

Although bark beetle outbreaks have occurred infrequently in whitebark pine forests in the past century, written, tree-ring, and fossil records indicate that during the late 1920s and 1930s, elevated temperatures and reduced precipitation were associated with widespread mountain pine beetle-caused whitebark pine mortality throughout the northern Rocky Mountains. Once temperatures cooled, the infestations subsided. With projected climate trends suggesting a long run of warm temperatures, however, today's severe beetle outbreaks show no sign of letting up.

Mountain Pine Beetle–Caused Mortality in High Elevation White Pines

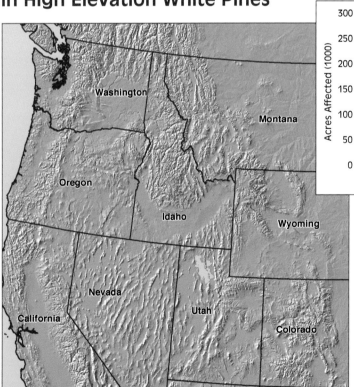

SOURCE: USDA FOREST SERVICE, FOREST HEALTH PROTECTION

More than 1.3 million acres of high elevation white pines (including whitebark pine, limber pine, and bristlecone pine) in the western United States have been affected by mountain pine beetle over the past 10 years. California is not included in these figures.

Mountain pine beetle–killed whitebark pine in Yellowstone National Park.

The Clark's nutcracker is one of a number of species that depend on the whitebark pine for survival.

These mountain pine beetle outbreaks come at a time when a non-native disease, white pine blister rust, has infected more than 65 percent of whitebark pine stands in the northern Rocky Mountains. Blister rust can reduce cone production, thereby limiting the number of new seeds available to renew those forests. When the infection is severe, the affected trees die as well. The combination of blister rust infection and bark beetle infestation is particularly troubling because bark beetles are killing trees that have developed genetic resistance to blister rust. The combination of blister rust and mountain pine beetle thwarts the potential benefits of natural selection. Resistant trees survive blister rust, but then succumb to mountain pine beetle. This one-two punch could mean the end of whitebark pine in parts of its range where both mountain pine beetles and blister rust are currently at high levels.

With so many trees dying, land managers and ecologists are developing restoration programs to prevent local and regional extinction of whitebark pine forests. Although it is impossible to suppress mountain pine beetle populations once they have become large enough to successfully colonize large numbers of trees in a stand, the direct, manual application of pesticides can protect individual, high-value trees from mountain pine beetle attack. Widespread pesticide application is not feasible over large areas, however, especially at the remote, high-elevation sites where whitebark pines are found. Synthetically produced pheromones, which mimic compounds naturally produced by the beetles, are easier to apply and can provide some protection against fatal bark beetle attacks, but have not proven consistently effective over several years.

Forestry professionals are also looking at long-term restoration efforts to develop whitebark pine communities that can weather the dual threats of blister rust and mountain pine beetle. Strategies include planting rust-resistant seedlings in areas where losses have been high, as well as stimulating natural regeneration of the stands. Allowing surface fires to burn in some affected whitebark pine stands can reduce competition with other vegetation and promote better growing conditions for those trees that survive the current outbreaks.

Blister rust is an exotic pathogen that infects five-needle pines.

Bark-beetle-caused tree mortality surrounding homes near Lake Arrowhead in southern California.

On the Kenai Peninsula in Alaska, for instance, where spruce beetle recently killed millions of trees over a relatively short period of time, native bluejoint grass has thrived in the now-open canopies. This ingrowth of grasses has been most pronounced in areas that were salvage-logged following the outbreak. Spruce trees may not be able to grow on many of these sites for hundreds of years, because the grass crowds out spruce seedlings as they regenerate. Outbreak areas that were not logged, however, sustained enough "nurse trees"—fallen trees that provide shelter for new seedlings—to foster a new cohort of spruce and other tree species.

Such rapid changes in forest composition also can affect wildlife species that have evolved to survive in specific habitats. Although some bird species rely on bark beetle-infested trees to nest and feed, other species depend on live trees. The Clark's nutcracker, for instance, feeds on whitebark pine seeds, which the birds hide away in thousands of caches to sustain them during lean times. Red squirrels also store large numbers of whitebark pine cones in middens on the forest floor, and grizzly and black bears regularly raid those middens to feed during the critical months prior to winter hibernation. Similarly, piñon pine seeds are vital food sources for many native mammals and birds in the southwestern U.S. When piñon pines experience mass mortality, the species that depend on them may decline as well.

In addition, massive tree mortality can affect watershed quality and quantity. Live trees in high-elevation watersheds provide shade and shelter that help to maintain the winter snowpack and prevent quick runoff during the spring melt and summer storms. Large numbers of bark beetle-killed trees within a watershed increase the risk of rapid snow loss and can enhance annual streamflow.

Live trees also provide aesthetic and recreational forest values, and wilderness tourism may decline as a consequence of massive bark beetle-kill events. A massive beetle kill on the slopes of ski resorts, for example, can result in earlier melting in spring and more drifting during wind events, compromising snow quality. In addition, bark beetle-killed trees may become "hazard trees" because once dead they are prone to falling, and require costly removal to keep backcountry trail networks and forest campgrounds safe and navigable.

Bark beetle outbreaks also can modify forest carbon balances. Mature forests store large amounts of carbon. When mature trees are killed by bark beetles, the stored carbon in the dead trees is released over several decades during decomposition. Thus, in the short term, forest carbon storage can be greatly reduced as the stored carbon is released. However, as new trees grow in the several decades following an outbreak, the net carbon flux (a measure of both decomposition and new growth) eventually shifts, and the forest again becomes a carbon sink, absorbing more carbon than it releases. An adequate estimate of the influence of bark beetle outbreaks on carbon balance requires consideration of multiple factors, including regeneration rates, the amount of time since the outbreak occurred, and the number and vigor of surviving trees. More research is needed to assess how changes in outbreak regimes might affect ecosystem carbon balances.

Bark Beetles and Fire

Bark beetles and fire are the two biggest natural disturbances in western North American forests, often—but not always—interacting to regenerate old stands. Fire ecologists are just beginning to understand the relationship between bark beetle-caused tree mortality and fire in those ecosystems they have studied. This relationship is extremely complex, and varies by location and forest type. Scientists use the term "fire hazard" to describe the probability of a fire occurring in a forest. "Fire hazard" refers to the state of the fuels in a given stand—the density of the overhead canopy and the amount and arrangement of ground and ladder fuels including grasses, shrubs, and small trees. Weather also influences fire behavior, but the term "fire hazard" refers specifically to the state of fuels independent of those variables such as temperature, wind, and precipitation that influence fuel moisture content.

Figure 10 is a generalized framework summarizing current knowledge of fire

Crown-fire hazard remains high in the year or two after a bark beetle outbreak, when dead needles remain on trees. After the needles drop, crown-fire hazard also falls.

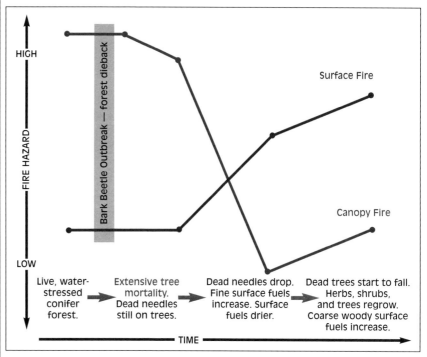

FIGURE 10.

Hypothesized Fire Hazard Following Bark Beetle Outbreaks

SOURCE: CRAIG ALLEN

Hypothesized changes in conifer forest fire hazard following a severe bark beetle outbreak assuming continuously dry climate conditions. Actual fire behavior will vary depending on many factors, including predominant climate and fire weather, landscape site factors (e.g., slope), and vegetation structure and species. We refer the reader to publications in the Additional Reading section for more detail on these complex relationships.

PHOTO BY JIM KAUTZ

Crown fires spread rapidly and can destroy large areas of forest.

hazard and fire behavior following a bark beetle outbreak and is based on field research and simulation model results. Both crown- and surface-fire hazard change through time following a bark beetle outbreak event in a stand of living conifers. For one to two years following a bark beetle outbreak, crown-fire hazard is expected to be high while dead needles remain on the tree, stocking the canopy with dry, fine fuels that can ignite quickly during weather conditions conducive to fire. After the dead needles fall and canopy fuel continuity is interrupted, crown-fire hazard declines markedly relative to pre-outbreak conditions. However, surface-fire hazard may increase in that period. Wind speed and solar input increase without the shade and shelter provided by the high canopy, drying out fine surface fuels such as the fallen needles from beetle-killed trees. Warmer, windier conditions also allow fires to spread more quickly and burn more intensely. Surface-fire hazard continues to increase once the dead trees fall, adding downed wood to the surface fuel load. Shrubs and young trees that grow in place of the bark beetle-killed trees also add to surface-fire hazard and serve as ladder fuels that can spread fire into tree crowns.

The effects of bark beetle outbreaks on subsequent fire hazard varies greatly depending on ecosystem type and initial stand conditions (e.g., understory and overstory composition, stand structure and age, and the number of standing and fallen dead trees). Generally speaking, crown- and surface-fire risks change with time following outbreaks, and factors such as weather and forest composition play large roles in determining whether and how intensely a fire will burn. Results from two studies illustrate these points.

Research into the effects of a spruce beetle outbreak in Colorado during the 1940s indicates that fire frequency was no greater in the half-century following the outbreak than in the years preceding it when compared with forests not affected by the spruce beetle outbreak (Figure 11). Widespread fires occur only an average of once every two centuries in high-elevation spruce forests, and are generally

FIGURE 11.

Fires in Colorado Following Spruce Beetle Outbreaks

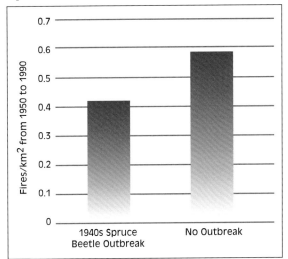

SOURCE: BEBI ET AL 2003

A large spruce beetle outbreak in the White River National Forest in Colorado during the 1940s had little influence on the number and size of subsequent fires.

The Yellowstone fires burned intensely both in areas where beetles had been active and in areas where they had not. Studies indicate that trees were slightly more likely to burn in areas where beetles had been active in an outbreak that occurred 15 years before the fires. However, an area that experienced an outbreak 5-10 years previous to the fires was less likely to burn.

dependent on extreme drought. Despite an increase in fire hazard following the 1940s outbreak, weather conditions were generally not conducive to extreme fire events during those years. Only during the severe drought of 2002 did those forests burn. When they did, both beetle-killed stands and stands unaffected by the spruce beetle burned in a similar fashion. These observations suggest that many of Colorado's high-elevation spruce-fir forests have burned not because of a large change in fuels following a spruce beetle outbreak, but because of "fire weather"— hot, dry, and windy conditions that promote acceleration of severe crown fires.

With Bark Beetles, One Size Does Not Fit All

The factors influencing a bark beetle outbreak vary depending on the species of bark beetle, geographic region, and host tree species.

Bark beetle outbreaks appear to have a more causal relationship with fire in other ecosystems, such as lodgepole pine forests in Yellowstone National Park. In the extensive Yellowstone fires of 1988, lodgepole pine forests that had been affected by a mountain pine beetle outbreak 15 years previous were more likely to burn than were nearby locations where bark beetles had not been active. Trees killed by an outbreak that had occurred only five to ten years previously, however, were not found to have contributed to the fire's spread or increased its intensity. This evidence indicates that, in the areas studied in Yellowstone, the release of understory "ladder fuels" years after a mass beetle-kill poses more of a fire risk than the short-term increase in dead fuel caused by a more recent outbreak. Although beetle-affected stands played varying roles in the Yellowstone fires, the principal reason why the fires were so intense was that weather conditions were extreme, with prolonged drought and high winds. Indeed, some forests without previous bark beetle activity burned as intensely as forests where beetles had been especially active.

If bark beetle outbreaks sometimes have an effect on forest fire hazard, the reverse is also true: forest fires can influence bark beetle activity. Although stand-replacing fires can reduce outbreak risk in the long-term by removing the large, mature trees that bark beetles prefer, in the short term, some species of bark beetles, in particular Douglas-fir beetle and western pine beetle, are attracted to trees that have been damaged, but not killed, by fire. Post-fire beetle attack by these species can kill up to 25 percent of trees that survive a forest fire—a factor that may need to be taken into account when considering the use of prescribed burns to promote forest health. We do not currently have sufficient information, however, to assess whether fire-injured trees can help foster the build-up of bark beetle populations to such an extent that they can attack and overcome healthy trees in the surrounding forests.

These studies help us understand the historical relationship between bark beetles and fire. As bark beetle outbreak dynamics shift—and we see levels of tree mortality that have not been observed in recent history—the dynamic relationship between fire and bark beetle disturbances also may change. Although beetle outbreaks and fire risk differ from forest to forest, historical fire and beetle activity are certainly linked in one respect: conditions that influence wildfires—warm temperatures, drought-stressed trees, and a dense forest canopy—also favor beetle activity.

Research Gaps

Although outbreaks in recent years have provided scientists with excellent opportunities to conduct studies and gather new information about the role of bark beetles in western forests, much research remains to be done. In addition to the gaps in our understanding discussed above, a number of bark beetle-related dynamics are still not fully understood.

- How different species of trees are affected by climate change, including seasonal shifts in precipitation, temperature, and increased atmospheric gases, and the indirect effect of these changes on tree resistance to attacking bark beetles.

- The degree to which the current beetle population explosions have been triggered by changes in climate such as drought and rising temperatures, versus forest habitat conditions such as overly dense or homogenous stands of trees.

- The impact of outbreaks on ecosystem processes such as forest fire, nutrient cycling, and forest regeneration, and how current changes in bark beetle outbreaks will affect these processes.

- How these dramatic new outbreaks will affect various landscapes, particularly those that have not previously, or have only rarely, experienced bark beetle outbreaks in recorded history.

- Whether various harvesting strategies, including thinning at large spatial scales prior to a beetle outbreak, reduce the probability and severity of an infestation in multiple forest types.

- The interplay between beetle outbreaks and invasion by non-native species. Do invasive plants such as cheatgrass, which has expanded into areas of widespread piñon mortality in the southwestern United States, thrive in areas that have been hard-hit by bark beetles?

- The economic and social impacts of bark beetle disturbance. How will large-scale outbreaks and massive tree mortality affect the forest-products and tourism industries and the communities that depend on them?

- How does the loss of habitat associated with bark beetle outbreaks affect wildlife—in particular threatened, sensitive, and endangered species?

Bark Beetles and Forest Management

The current bark beetle outbreaks, and the vast numbers of dead trees these outbreaks leave behind, present difficult challenges for managers and policymakers. Multiple factors—such as stand type, local conditions, bark beetle population level, and resource and community objectives—must be considered before making landscape-scale management decisions in forests affected or threatened by bark beetle infestations.

For example, it may make sense to use insecticides on high-value trees on a small scale, such as in campgrounds or around homes, but such spraying is not feasible on a large landscape scale. In some instances, strategies such as thinning may be effective prior to a large outbreak to reduce competition among trees, thereby enhancing the health and defensive capacity of individual trees. This strategy, however, is less effective once bark beetle populations have grown so large that they can overcome the defenses of even the healthiest trees. In addition, populations of certain bark beetle species, such as those within the genus *Ips* can in some instances reproduce and proliferate in logging debris that thinning operations leave behind. Moreover, some environmental triggers, such as unusually warm weather, may override all attempts to prevent a successful colonization event. Once an outbreak reaches landscape scale, no known management options are effective or practical for stopping the outbreak.

Evaluating the appropriate management response to a bark beetle disturbance event requires understanding not only the complexities of local and regional ecology—the species-specific, cross-scale interactions occurring within the forested landscape—but also the long-term influence of these management actions on the surrounding landscape. For example, in the wildland-urban interface where homes have been built near forest boundaries, land managers may experience pressure to remove beetle-killed trees to reduce perceived fire risk and lessen the visual impact of so many dead trees. Although removing dead trees and other fuel has been shown to reduce fire risk in the immediate vicinity of a home and is advisable under many circumstances, the link between bark beetle outbreaks and subsequent fire at the larger landscape scale is not fully understood. In addition, the role mechanical thinning should play in fire reduction is unresolved and varies depending on the location and type of forest. Although conventional harvesting usually targets the largest timber for removal, recent research suggests that in some ecosystems, the removal of small trees, brush, and ground fuels that carry a fire may actually be more effective in reducing fire risk.

The changing dynamics of current outbreaks make management decisions even more difficult. Some outbreaks have no recent precedent, so an appropriate management response can not necessarily be formulated based on previous events. One important aspect of future forest management will be an evaluation of multiple approaches across a range of spatial scales and outbreak severity levels. Many areas will regenerate naturally following a bark beetle outbreak and require no action. In some areas severely affected by recent outbreaks, land managers may want to consider the creation of a diverse forest through modifications to species and age classes at a regional scale. In addition, some ecosystems that have highly susceptible forest conditions, but are currently unaffected by bark beetles, may benefit from actions to reduce stand density. This is particularly true in lodgepole and ponderosa pine stands where research has shown that thinning can reduce susceptibility. Finally, policymakers and forestry professionals should incorporate projections of climate-change induced stress on host forests and direct effects of warming temperature on bark beetle populations when developing future forest management strategies.

Additional Reading

Allen, C.D. 2007. Cross-scale interactions among forest dieback, fire, and erosion in northern New Mexico landscapes. *Ecosystems* 10:797–808.

Aukema, B.H, A.L. Carroll, Y. Zheng, J. Zhu, K.F. Raffa, R.D. Moore, K. Stahl, and S.W. Taylor. 2008. Movement of outbreak populations of mountain pine beetle: Influences of spatiotemporal patterns and climate. *Ecography* 31:348–358.

Bebi, P., D. Kulakowski, and T.T. Veblen. 2003. Interactions between fire and spruce beetle in a subalpine Rocky Mountain forest landscape. *Ecology* 84:362–371.

Bentz, B.J., J.A. Logan, and G.D. Amman. 1991. Temperature dependent development of the mountain pine beetle (Coleoptera: Scolytidae), and simulation of its phenology. *The Canadian Entomologist* 123:1083–1094.

Bentz, B.J., J.A. Logan, and J.C. Vandygriff. 2001. Latitudinal life history variation in *Dendroctonus ponderosae* (Coleoptera: Scolytidae) development time and size. *The Canadian Entomologist* 133:375–387.

Berg, E.E., J.D. Henry, C.L. Fastie, A.D. De Volder, and S.M. Matsuoka. 2006. Spruce beetle outbreaks on the Kenai Peninsula, Alaska, and Kluane National Park and Reserve, Yukon Territory: Relationship to summer temperatures and regional differences in disturbance regimes. *Forest Ecology and Management* 227:219–232.

Bigler, C., D. Kulakowski, and T.T. Veblen. 2005. Multiple disturbance interactions and drought influence fire severity in Rocky Mountain subalpine forests. *Ecology* 86:30183029.

Breshears, D.D., O.B. Myers, C.W. Meyer, F.J. Barnes, C.B. Zou, C.D. Allen, N.G. McDowell, and W.T. Pockman. (In press). Tree die-off in response to global-change-type drought: Mortality insights from a decade of plant water potential measurements. *Frontiers in Ecology and the Environment.* DOI:10.1890/080016.

Brunelle, A., G. Rehfeldt, B. Bentz, and S. Munson. 2008. Holocene records of *Dendroctonus* bark beetles in high elevation pine forests of Idaho and Montana, USA. *Forest Ecology and Management* 255:836–846.

Cardoza, Y.J., K.D. Klepzig, and K.F. Raffa. 2006. Bacteria in oral secretions of an endophytic insect inhibit antagonistic fungi. *Ecological Entomology* 31:636–645.

Fettig, C.J., K.D. Klepzig, R.F. Billings, A.S. Munson, T.E. Nebeker, J.F. Negrón, and J.T. Nowak. 2007. The effectiveness of vegetation management practices for prevention and control of bark beetle infestations in coniferous forests of the western and southern United States. *Forest Ecology and Management* 238:24–53.

Greenwood, D.L., and P.J. Weisberg. 2008. Density-dependent tree mortality in pinyon-juniper woodlands. *Forest Ecology and Management* 255:2129–2137.

Hansen, E.M., B.J. Bentz, and D.L. Turner. 2001. Temperature-based model for predicting univoltine brood proportions in spruce beetle (Coleoptera: Scolytidae). *The Canadian Entomologist* 133:827–841.

Hicke, J.A. and J.C. Jenkins. 2008. Mapping lodgepole pine stand structure susceptibility to mountain pine beetle attack across the western United States. *Forest Ecology and Management* 225:1536–1547.

Hicke, J.A., J.A. Logan, J. Powell, and D.S. Ojima. 2006. Changing temperatures influence suitability for modeled mountain pine beetle (*Dendroctonus ponderosae*) outbreaks in the western United States. *Journal of Geophysical Research-Biogeosciences* 111, G02019, DOI:02010.01029/02005JG000101.

IPCC. 2001. *Climate change 2001: The scientific basis.* Contribution of Working Group 1 to the Third Assessment Report of the Intergovernmental Panel on Climate Change. Cambridge University Press, Cambridge, New York, USA.

IPCC. 2007. *Climate change 2007: The scientific basis.* Contribution of Working Group 1 to the Fourth Assessment Report of the Intergovernmental Panel on Climate Change. Cambridge University Press, Cambridge, New York, USA.

Jenkins, M.J., E. Hebertson, W. Page, and C.A. Jorgersen. 2008. Bark beetles, fuels, fire and implications for forest management in the Intermountain West. *Forest Ecology and Management.* 254:16–34.

Jones, M.E., T.D. Paine, M.E. Fenn, and M.A. Poth. 2004. Influence of ozone and nitrogen deposition on bark beetle activity under drought conditions. *Forest Ecology and Management* 200:67–76.

Kulakowski, D. and T.T. Veblen. 2007. Effect of prior disturbances on the extent and severity of a 2002 wildfire in Colorado subalpine forests. *Ecology* 88:759–769.

Kurz, W.A., C.C. Dymond, G. Stinson, G.J. Rampley, E.T. Neilson, A.L. Carroll, T. Ebata, and L. Safranyik. 2008. Mountain pine beetle and forest carbon feedback to climate change. *Nature* 452:987–990, DOI:10.1038/nature06777.

Lynch, H.J., R.A. Renkin, R.L. Crabtree, and P.R. Moorcroft. 2006. The influence of previous mountain pine beetle (*Dendroctonus ponderosae*) activity on the 1988 Yellowstone fires. *Ecosystems* 9:1318–1327.

Logan, J.A. and J.A. Powell. 2001. Ghost forests, global warming, and the mountain pine beetle. *American Entomologist* 47:160–173.

Logan, J.A. and J.A. Powell. (In Press). Ecological consequences of climate change altered forest insect disturbance regimes. In F.H. Wagner (ed.), *Climate change in western North America: Evidence and environmental effects.* Allen Press.

Maroja, L.S., S.M. Bogdanowicz, K.F. Wallin, K.F. Raffa, and R.G. Harrison. 2007. Phylogeography of spruce beetles (*Dendroctonus rufipennis* Kirby) (Curculionidae: Scolytinae) in North America: Distinctive mtDNA lineages associated with different species of host trees. *Molecular Ecology* 16:2560–2573.

McDowell, N., W.T. Pockman, C.D. Allen, D.D. Breshears, N. Cobb, T. Kolb, J. Sperry, A. West, D. Williams, and E.A.Yepez. 2008. Mechanisms of plant survival and mortality during drought: Why do some plants survive while others succumb to drought? Tansley Review, *New Phytologist,* DOI:10.1111/j.1469-8137.2008.02436.

Mock, K.E., B.J. Bentz, E.M. O'Neill, J. P. Chong, J. Orwin, and M.E. Pfrender. 2007. Landscape-scale genetic variation in a forest outbreak species, the mountain pine beetle (*Dendroctonus ponderosae*). *Molecular Ecology* 16:553–568.

Negrón, J.F. and J.B. Popp. 2004. Probability of ponderosa pine infestation by mountain pine beetle in the Colorado Front Range. *Forest Ecology and Management* 191:17–27.

Negrón, J.F., K.K. Allen, B. Cook, and J.R.Withrow Jr. 2008. Susceptibility of ponderosa pine, *Pinus ponderosa* (Dougl. ex Laws.), to mountain pine beetle, *Dendroctonus ponderosae* Hopkins, attack in uneven-aged stands in the Black Hills of South Dakota and Wyoming USA. *Forest Ecology and Management* 254:327–334.

Paine, T.D., K.F. Raffa, and T.C. Harrington. 1997. Interactions among scolytid bark beetles, their associated fungi, and live host conifers. *Annual Review of Entomology* 42:179–206.

Powell, J.A. and J.A. Logan. 2005. Insect seasonality-circle map analysis of temperature-driven life cycles. *Theoretical Population Biology* 67:161–179.

Raffa, K.F. and A.A. Berryman. 1982. Physiological differences between lodgepole pines resistant and susceptible to the mountain pine beetle and associated microorganisms. *Environmental Entomology* 11:486–492.

Raffa, K.F. and D.L. Dahlsten. 1995. Differential responses among natural enemies and prey to bark beetle pheromones. *Oecologia* 102:17–23.

Raffa, K.F., B.H. Aukema, B.J. Bentz, A.L. Carroll, J.A. Hicke, M.G. Turner, and W.H. Romme. 2008. Cross-scale drivers of natural disturbances prone to anthropogenic amplification: Dynamics of biome-wide bark beetle eruptions. *BioScience* 58(6):501–518.

Régnière J. and B. Bentz. 2007. Modeling cold tolerance in the mountain pine beetle, *Dendroctonus ponderosae*. *Journal of Insect Physiology* 53:559–572.

Régnière J. and R. St-Amant. 2007. Stochastic simulation of daily air temperature and precipitation from monthly normals in North America north of Mexico. *International Journal of Biometeorology* 51:415–430.

Romme, W.H., J. Clement, J. Hicke, D. Kulakowski, L.H. MacDonald, T.L. Schoennagel, and T.T. Veblen. 2006. Recent forest insect outbreaks and fire risk in *Colorado forests: A brief synthesis of relevant research*. Colorado Forest Restoration Institute, Report, 24 pp. Fort Collins, CO.

Safranyik, L. and B. Wilson. 2006. *The mountain pine beetle: A synthesis of biology, management, and impacts on lodgepole pine*. Natural Resources Canada, Canadian Forest Service, Pacific Forestry Centre, Victoria, BC. Available at: http://bookstore.cfs.nrcan.gc.ca/

Safranyik, L., D.M. Shrimpton, H.S. Whitney. 1975. An interpretation of the interaction between lodgepole pine, the mountain pine beetle and its associated blue stain fungi in western Canada. Pages 406-428. In D.M. Baumgartner (ed), *Management of lodgepole pine ecosystems.* Washington State University Cooperative Extension Service, Pullman, WA.

Schwandt, J. 2006. *Whitebark pine in peril: A case for restoration.* USDA Forest Service, Forest Health Protection, R1-06-28, Coeur d'Alene, Idaho, U.S.A.

Seybold, S.J., D.P.W. Huber, J.C. Lee, A.D. Graves, and J. Bohlmann. 2006. Pine monoterpenes and pine bark beetles: a marriage of convenience for defense and chemical communication. *Phytochemical Reviews* 5:143–178.

Sibold, J.S., T.T. Veblen, K. Chipko, L. Lawson, E. Mathis, and J. Scott. 2007. Influences of secondary disturbances on lodgepole pine stand development in Rocky Mountain National Park. *Ecological Applications* 17:1638–1655.

Six, D.L. and Adams, J. 2007. White pine blister rust severity and selection of individual whitebark pine by the mountain pine beetle (Coleoptera: Curculionidae, Scolytinae). *Journal of Entomological Science* 42:345–353.

Six, D.L. and B.J. Bentz. 2007. Temperature determines the relative abundance of symbionts in a multipartite bark beetle-fungus ectosymbiosis. *Microbial Ecology* 54:112–118.

Taylor, S.W. and A.L. Carroll. 2004. Disturbance, forest age dynamics and mountain pine beetle outbreaks in BC: A historical perspective. Pages 41-51. In Shore, T.L., J.E. Brooks, and J.E. Stone (eds), *Challenges and Solutions: Proceedings of the Mountain Pine Beetle Symposium.* Kelowna, British Columbia, Canada October 30–31, 2003. Canadian Forest Service, Pacific Forestry Centre, Information Report BC-X-399. 287 p. Available at: http://bookstore.cfs.nrcan.gc.ca/

Tomback, D.F. and P. Achuff. (In Press). Blister rust and western forest biodiversity: Ecology, values, and outlook for five-needled white pines. *Forest Pathology.*

Tomback, D.F., S.F. Arno, and R.E. Keane. 2001. The compelling case for management intervention. Pages 3-25. In Tomback, D.F., S.F. Arno, R.E. Keane (eds), *Whitebark pine communities: Ecology and Restoration.* Washington, D.C.: Island Press.

Tran, J.K., T. Ylioja, R. Billings, J. Régnière, and M.P. Ayres. 2007. Impact of minimum winter temperatures on the population dynamics of *Dendroctonus frontalis* (Coleoptera: Scolytinae). *Ecological Applications* 17:882–899.

Veblen, T.T., K.S. Hadley, M.S. Reid, and A.J. Rebertus. 1991. The response of subalpine forests to spruce beetle outbreak in Colorado. *Ecology* 72:213-231.

Veblen, T.T., K.S. Hadley, E.M. Nel, T. Kitzberger, M. Reid, and R. Villalba. 1994. Disturbance regime and disturbance interactions in a Rocky Mountain subalpine forest. *Journal of Ecology* 82:125-135.

Wood, D.L. 1982. The role of pheromones, kairomones, and allomones in the host selection and colonization behavior of bark beetles. *Annual Review of Entomology* 27:411-446.